PERSEPHONE'S GARDEN

Persephone's Garden

Printed in China.

ISBN-13: 978-0-9991935-6-3
ISBN-10: 0-9991935-6-2

SA 044

Library of Congress Number: 2019931010

Published by Secret Acres
200 Park Avenue South, 8th fl.
New York, NY 10003

Some comics in this book were previously published in the Strumpet 5, InkBrick, Spiralbound, Popula, the NewYorker.com, and MuthaMagazine.com

THANK YOU
to Leon for seeing the possibility of this book and making it happen. Thank you to John Franklin ♡ and to Sylvan and Helen for keeping our lives lively. Thanks to my parents, especially my dad, Tom Fawkes, for taking care of my mother. I'm grateful to friends Summer Pierre, Jennifer Hayden, and Ellen Lindner, and to James Sturm and the Center for Cartoon Studies for inspiration. Thanks also to la Maison des Auteurs for a month-long residency in 2018 where I wrote some of the comics included here.

E SE HONE'S GARDEN

Persephone's Garden is not a place of Greek myth– It's an invention for this collection of comics and drawings that span the years 2012–2018, a large part of my children's' childhood.

Persephone, in the *Homeric Hymn to Demeter*, was walking in a flowery meadow when she caught sight of a dazzling 100-headed flower.

It was a lure; when she reached for it, the earth gave way, Hades in his chariot snatched her and took her to the Underworld.

Demeter heard her daughter's scream, but had no idea what had happened, and searched for nine days and nights.

Then she sat down in anger and refused to let anything grow, grieving for her lost child. Until Zeus allowed Persephone to visit.

Of course the story is connected to the seasons of the natural world, but also allows readers to recognize our own losses, separations, grief.

When I was young and first read the story, I felt like Persephone, picking flowers and wary of the danger of being caught.

Now I'm also Demeter, anticipating inevitable separation from the children – as they grow up – though fear of worse is never far.

Persephone's time spent walking in the flowery meadow was short, as are the months when she returns to earth. She is fleeting,

as are many of the comics in this book. Many began as sketchbook drawings, as well as travel diaries from Israel and Greece.

Diary comics became an exercise in composition and distillation, catching the essence of what the Kids did and said a way of discovering the humor and ridiculousness of life.

But it's not so funny for the Kids now! They request that I not draw them anymore. Too bad! They say the darndest things!

Subject line of an email from one of the Kids after a comic was published on line.

Meanwhile, my mother, keeper of memories of my own childhood, has Alzheimers, and almost all her memory is gone.

It's as if Hades has come for her already, but has left her body. Her ability to create, to take care of herself, and to know her family are all gone.

She's as lost in the dark as Persephone. So here is this book of comics about small, potentially forgettable events of daily life—

—of bedtime conversations, food disputes, homework troubles, and the whims of talking rabbits—

—as beams of Demeter's torches—

On 5th C. Athenian vases, Demeter appears with two torches, emblems of her search.

—trying to capture how we were at certain moments even as things change and slide away into darkness.

TROIA

When I sat at my desk under a tent on the site of Troy drawing pottery for two months in 2001, I dreamed of the events of the Iliad that had taken place on the same ground. Richard McGuire's book *Here* inspired these drawings.

More to draw.
Don't Listen!

Ships!
Can you work a little faster?

CHOMP
Strongest walls
YOW!

These need some corrections.
Have some Pringles.
Antiklos! Diomedes! Odysseus!

Flies!
It has a higher curve on The base.

Early 5th century.
Later 5th c. See the difference?
Sob

Or work an extra hour a day?
Already working 11.
Waaaa!

Recently I saw my mother's tapestries in a dream.

For most of my life she wove large-scale tapestries in linen for gallery shows and national commissions.

She drew on graph paper first, planning the compositions according to the geometry of the warp and weft.

She created shimmering and dazzling effects with color from the parallel and diagonal lines of the grid.

In the last few years, the gradual effects of Alzheimer's has taken away her abilities to draw, plan, and weave.

My dad sent me the last of her graph paper.

In a dream, I watched her once meticulous structures dissolve into dissonant abstractions, until they faded to blank.

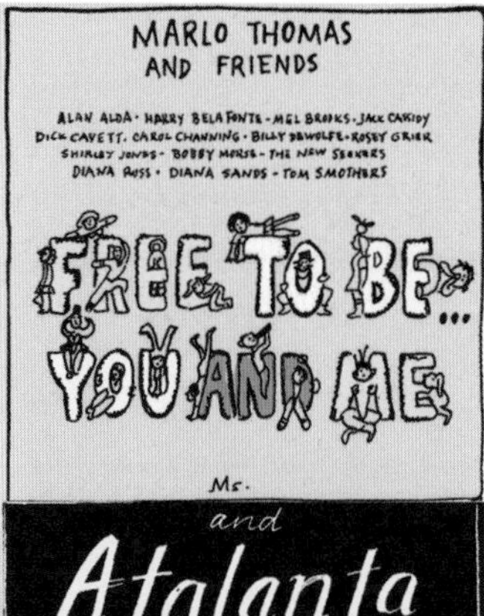

and

Atalanta

GLYNNIS FAWKES in 2017.

especially Atalanta.

She was so bright and so clever that many young men wished to marry her.

I will hold a great race. The winner will have the right to marry Atalanta.

I'm not sure I want to marry anyone! But if there's a race I want to run too.

I forgot all about Free To Be... You and Me until I found it again a few years ago.
Hey Kids! Here's something you'll like!
FREE

We put that CD right on.
There's a land that I see...

I wasn't ready for the flood of emotions at hearing the songs again.
where the children are free...

Every boy in this land... Grows to be his own man...
Choke!
Mama! Stop Singing so we can hear!
Yeah!

Every girl in this land... Grows to be her own woman...
Gulp, that's ME.
I was a girl, and grew up.
I'm my own woman, even.
Somehow I didn't really notice until now.

I felt time collapse 35 years to when I knew these songs by heart, songs ringing with optimism for gender equality...
This is where my feminism comes from, before I'd ever heard the word.
"Hi! I'm a baby!" "What do you think I am, a loaf of bread?"

...that seems just as necessary in the darkness of NOW. They're catchy, too! Although they do show their age.
"Yuck! A bald girl! Disgusting!" ... "Here comes the nurse to change our diapers..."
How's Atalanta been doing after all this time?
Haha Babies!

I read the myth in the Library of Apollodorus. There was a race, but Atalanta was duped by a suitor and had to marry him.
But for me, she'll always be one of the few girls in Greek myth who got away.
Haha Diapers!

Keep running, Atalanta! Keep running, all girls, and be free!
Chase me, mama!
Chase me too!

WOODS HOLE

MILL pond
OUR HOUSE
CHURCH
MILLFIELD STREET
QUISSETT
CRICKET LANE
SWOPE
Eel pond
MARINE BIOLOGICAL LAB
STORE
CAPTAIN KIDD
STREET
SCHOOL
SCHOOL STREET
WOODS HOLE OCEANOGRAPHIC EXHIBIT CENTER
COMMUNITY HALL
COFFEE O.
WCAI
TO FALMO
PIE IN THE SKY
WOODS HOLE PUBLIC LIBRARY
BUS STOP
TO NO
STEAMSHIP AUTHORITY

WOODS HOLE
MASSACHUSETTS
41.5245° N
70.6710° W
BUZZARDS BAY
WOODS HOLE
My husband
John grew up
in Woods Hole
in an apartment
above a shop
on Water Street.

CAPE
COD
BAY
ATLANTIC OCEAN
NANTUCKET
SOUND
Glynnis Fawkes 2014

To go to school, he walked up Water Street past the Community Hall,
over the Eelpond lift bridge, and cut past some docks.

If you keep going past the school and turn left onto Millfield St, you reach the Church and its garden.

You can see the buildings of Woods Hole
Oceanographic and the Marine Biological
Laboratories across Eel Pond.

At the end of Millfield St. is the house we lived in The year our son was born.
After an ocean flood a few years earlier, the house was raised up a storey.

Behind the house is
Mill pond and the
cottage where we
sometimes stay when
we come back to visit.

During the winter we lived there, storm winds howled over the roof

so fiercely
I was afraid
the roof
would blow
off.
The baby matched the
wind in howling all night
long.

In the day, I look the baby walking around Eel pond...

...and around past
Nobska lighthouse.

He would jump and shout for joy at the rushing waves and wind.

Going away in two days.

And from John's BIG Body too!

IS IT WORTH IT?

Before travelling, Images of where I'm going flash into my mind.
Sound of cicadas
Rooms Marinos & view of AkroCorinth

I'm anticipating the view of Mt. Hymetos from the plane
with all those antennae on top.
I climbed it once (the Mt. & an antenna)

And the sun of Greece that is so bright after the long trip.
T°METRO ΠΡΟΣ
ΠΡΟΑΣΤΙΑΚΟ

and that feeling of exhaustian and Jetlag combined with the thrill and fascination of being there.
on the train to Corinth.

Middle-Aged Maenad☆

☆A female follower of Dionysos

I first came to Greece when I was 27.

I wrote my undergrad honors Thesis on Maenads and Satyrs on Archaic Athenian Vases.

But I still associate being in Greece with my adventurous youth.

AIRPORT
PURGATORY

Waiting around like this makes me wonder what time is worth, anyway.
G 19

Other people are playing games, reading, on the phone, staring into space.
DELAYS
So I sayz, No way. Yeah I'm in The airport
TWO stations of KLASSIC HITS playing at once

If I was at home, I could be working on something big and listening to the BBC.
Riders on the Storm... Killer on the road...

And uploading comics, posting on FB & twitter, reading the internet...
Lonely Luggage wagon
At least ~~I'm not~~ making any less money than I would be if I was home.

TURBULANCE

The plane from Burlington tried to land in Philadelphia, but a foot above the runway it tipped sideways because of windsheer and climbed back in the sky, circled around to try again—
So, I missed the direct flight to Athens and was wobbly in the knees.

MY BODY CAME WITH ME TO GREECE

ARRIVED IN ANCIENT CORINTH – IMPRESSED BY THE STUDENTS WITH PHONES

At Breakfast & on the bus – how WIFI changes everything. Where's the banter of yore?

MARINOS ROOMS

waiting for dinner time.

MARINOS ROOMS
BED & BREAKFAST
TRADITIONAL GREEK HOSPITALITY
ΤΑΒΕΡΝΑ-ΕΣΤΙΑΤΟΡΙΟ

Back in Archaia Corinth:

View from the hotel reveals itself slowly:

an orange grove with a herd of sheep,
shepherd's moped, two barking puppies, the shepherd.

Tour of our Room

View from tiny window:

Sound of plumbing, mopeds, & cooing doves.

Akrocorinth with medieval fortress on top & Chimney of preschool nextdoor.

WHAT I MISS

MY BED AT HOME
This bed is as hard as plywood. I can feel the bones in my knees scraping

and it's cold! I'm wearing my scarf and 2 shirts.

It's narrow— only room for me—

and no Johnny mou!

WILDLIFE OF AKROCORINTH

BIG JUMP GRASSHOPPERS

FOLLOWING BUTTERFLY

ATTACK SPIDER WITH RED SPOTS

BLACK SNAKE AS THICK AS MY ARM

SILVER SNAKE WITH PALE GREEN STRIPE

BOTH QUICKLY SLITHERED AWAY INTO THE GRASS.

NEAR THE THEATRE AT CORINTH

The American School Dig house at Corinth

MY FIRST DIG & HOW I GOT INTO THE ILLUSTRATION RACKET

A local shepherd "forgot his watch" every day I was working in the cave.
* dovecote

JUST THE BEGINNING...

Though This was not The most interesting work, I was hooked on The life style of The dig and of Cyprus.

My 30th birthday under stars & grapes in a Cypriot village.

I drew on many projects over the next few years. Look out for my book about it!

WHY?

Now you may wonder why there is a need for archaeological drawing at all.
Aren't photos enough?
for Tuyeres maybe!

No! The drawings provide exact measurements which when they are published in the site reports allows comparisons between different sites and contexts within the site itself.
This one is 1cm thicker & 3cms longer and from a later context
This one needed more airflow for more copper?

Where the drawings are really relevent is with pottery.
Front view
profile + interior
Because pottery shapes and styles are diagnostic of the time and place they are made, the context and exact shape can tell a lot about the place they are found.

But of course most pottery - by far the most commonly found artefact in Mediterranean archaeology - is in broken fragments.
maybe a 2nd C. Roman Eastern Sigillata bowl?
From a sherd like this, I can make a drawing that will reconstruct the type of vessel & its diameter.
Nice for wine or barley porridge!

Or a mix!

NOT A BEACH DAY

TODAY I DREW POTTERY SOLIDLY FROM 8:30 TIL 3 WITH A SHORT BREAK AT 2:30 FOR LUNCH WITH THE GUYS.

BURP! Exqueeze me!

Done with This one? Here's some more from box 9.

LUNCH:

Chios chocolate, flavored with mastic.

TAKE ME TO THE BEACH!

OVER IT

I'm sure he does too— he is the director after all.

A HIKE UP AKROCORINTH
with Alice and what we talked about.

HIPPY
ARTIST-TYPE MOM

SOROROTY GIRLS

KENCHREAI PROJECT

CHACO SANDALS

They're expensive - That probably appeals to Them. And all Those cute colors!

No where else would I have The chance to hang out with so many fellow Chaco wearers - except maybe at the Farmer's market in Burlington?

NOW YOU KNOW WHAT TO WEAR AT THE ANCIENT HARBOR OF LECHION

AFTERNOON AT LECHION BEACH

view across Corinthian Gulf to Perachora

mother and daughter playing mermaids

Dan and Manuel with frappes

A View in each direction on Lechion Beach

toward ancient Lechion & harbor mole

toward modern Corinth & the Corinth Canal

10PM CONVERSATION WITH THE HEROIC WOMAN WHO OWNS THE MAIN GROCERY STORE IN ARCHAIA CORINTH.

I've talked with her every year and we have the same conversation each time.

BACK AT THE SUPERMARKET

ALL The QUESTIONS & ANSWERS

that happen in all the shops

You're American? Archaeologist?

I work with The archaeologists- I draw what They find.

Where do you stay?

Here in The village- Rooms Marinos

You work at Corinth?

No, Kenchriae but The Apotheke* is in Kyros Vrysi.

*Storage & work space.

Why do you speak Greek? Are you Greek-American?

No- I lived for 3 years in Cyprus- but my Greek isn't very good! I need practice!

Maybe you'll come back next year?

Maybe! This is my 5th year here! But There has to be money from The project and my family has to Let me go! So I hope so!

SONG IN THE SHOP – on Greek radio

This comes to 12€

Δευτερα Προγραμμα

I have a 20€.

Shsh!

Stop and listen to this song.

Rembetica

I bought some windchimes and salad tongs

This song is about a mother- she worries every time her children go out fishing

The boats weren't like boats today-

She never knew if they would return.

goose bump.

but got a Rembetika song from the 1930s.

WINDY

YESTERDAY WAS VERY WINDY.
WOOOOOOOO WOOOOO..
CHOOO
Bless you!
Thanks! The wind makes me sneeze!
WOOOOOO
LATER WE WENT TO THE BEACH.
wow! these waves are like Hawaii!
you're not going in, are you?
Let's go sit inside - too windy out here.
WHO's coming in?
Are you crazy?
too COLD!
I've got to catch up on my naps.

SURFIN ELLADA

QUIET DAY AT THE BEACH

LUNCH IN NAUPLIO

Lots of Kids everywhere!

As soon as you left, that Kid started to howl again–

Then the mother Started in! She Kept asking him "Why are you crying?"

Then she said, "theleis na phaeis Xilo?"–"you want to eat wood?"

Then she said That she'd never take him to The beach again!

And that She'd hit him! That's why I'm here early! She was worse than the Kid!

Sorry I missed That!

LAST DAY OF WORK

Walking down from signing in in the Isthmia museum to the Apotheke where we work - 8AM

HOW YOU GET TO ATHENS — IF YOU CAN

The Mystery of the Suburban train network on a Saturday.

HOW'S IT GOING?

A visit with my friend Anthoulla in Athens.

ON THE PAYPHONE IN THE VILLAGE

CORINTH TRAIN STATION 7.30 AM JUNE 6.
WAITING FOR THE TRAIN TO THE AIRPORT
ON THE LONG WAY BACK HOME.

On the train

YOU MIGHT THINK THE TRAIN WAS A VERY SUNNY PLACE

TWO WOMEN ACROSS FROM ME ON THE TRAIN

and their tremendous hair.

ATHENS AIRPORT MEMORIES

Here is the row of smarte carts I slept behind when I had an overnight layover between Kythera & London.

Here are the windows I said goodbye to John in front of after our 5 days in Santorini before we were together in 2003.

Goodbye hills of Attica and familiar yet mysterious airport buildings!

FLIGHT 743 to Philadelphia

HOME, HOME, HOME, HOME

In Greece, I'm an illustrator: a very specialized skill.

at home... I mainly clean, and not very well.

I'm hungry.

In Greece we're served dinner under the pines.

Ode to Joy

"Little witch Girl's Birthday"

ZZZZ ok That's all for tonight...
Mama! Get off my bed so I can get in!

Or I'll have to spank "Ode to Joy" on your butt!
ZZZZ

smak smack smak
smak smack smksmk
smak smak
ZZZZ
ow ow ow ow

In January 2012, we went to Israel so John could take up a 5-month fellowship at the Albright Institute in Jerusalem.

We arrived in Israel in the middle of the night— & had to spend an extra half-hour while they asked John what he was doing, where & why.

10 years ago, I made The same request—no problem—they gave me a stamped piece of paper that I could ditch before I went to Lebanon, Syria, Jordan, & Egypt.

This time they gave us a 1-month visa instead of The usual 3-month tourist visa. Because the official guessed my intent—or was it our East Jerusalem address?

This would mean an excursion to The East Jerusalem visa office/bunker in February.

We took a shared taxi from The airport into Jerusalem.

I was trying to glimpse familiar landmarks—Jaffa Gate, Damascus Gate.

Children's exhausted faces in Those amber street lights.

The next day we got up to explore - exhausted, jet-lagged with a cold in my head.

Our street, the way to Damascus Gate, everything seemed so intimidating.

We need to buy stuff - laundry soap, and -

youre going to go in a shop?

no, I'm too scared!

gold dome of The Dome of The Rock

Until I figure out what this money means! Maybe we can find a supermarket?

We did - in The Old City - but after This I went to these shops on Sultan Suleiman often.

I'm hungry!

We had hot lakhmajun & fresh orange juice in a place off Suk Khan-Ezzeit in The Christian Quarter. They were playing Fairuz, & I felt at home. We talked to the owner about music.

We also found a shop & spent a while marveling at The laundry soap & Kinds of KAAK — sort of crackers.

The first month in Jerusalem there was no help with the kids. John worked in the library, and I tried homeschooling.

Hey, Look! It's MATH TIME!

go away- were busy

FUN WITH MATH

Come on! You don't want to get behind in your class!

I'll help you- It will be fun! For each page you can earn points!

FUN WITH MATH ★

This is Kai's torture grind machine & here are the skeletons getting forked into the hopper.

Let's just do ONE PAGE and then have a snack!

NO FUN MATH

MAMA! NO! I'm not doing it ever- for anything!

So every day ended

not again!

WAAAAAAA

Daddy, watch me jump! Helen, watch out, I'm jumping

Can I make it until September?

school →

It's only 6 months!

I might actually hate the kids!
I'm a failure!
I'm no good!
I can't do anything!

I wasn't getting anything done. The kids refused to do "homeschool". It was freezing cold & grey. We went to every site & museum I thought the kids could handle.

Luckily, my parents came for a visit. Then, Brittany & Brendan, former students of John, came to stay in order to take care of the kids. Each had them for 3 hours, five days a week. I was SAVED.

Come on! Lets make cookies! Read a book! play legos!

Bye!

Mama mama

So I had time to work on the illustrations for John's book, some of my own projects, and this sketchbook. Here follows my record of this time....

SO DIFFICULT TO GO OUT!
Come on, Thomas it's an adventure!
ALBRIGHT
NO NO NO NO
NO NO NO NO
I'm NOT GOING! I'm going back home! I hate the old city and I'm never going there again in my whole life! It's all dark & crowded like a prison!
We aren't going to the Old City - we're going on the tram to a museum.
A museum? NO! I hate museums!
We're NOT GOING.
This one has special stuff for kids!
I hate kids stuff!
We are, actually
I ONLY want to go to a playground or to Bethlehem!
That's too far for today!
MAMA! Hurry up! We don't want to miss the tram! Here it comes!
Oooh, I love the tram!

After a good time in The museum.
Does This bus go to town?
King George St.
A Rabbi held Thomas's hand on The bus.

NABLOUS ROAD
ECOLE BIBLIQ
Thomas, was that a fun day? It was fun, wasn't it!
Yeah, it was fun!
Can I have it in *writing*?
No, he can't write.
I'll draw up a contract.

Dumpster cat.

On the way to the closest playground, which was all broken-down & strewn with broken glass.

Cats think it's feeding time.
A lot of cats lived in our yard,
but were feral & refused to be petted.
Hisham the cook fed them leftovers.

It rained all day & the kids were going crazy— not just the kids. I took them to the bakery where they skated on the floor & Helen fell down & I bought some sweet pastries & what turned out to be zaatar sesame sticks.— maybe whole wheat, maybe not.

paper-thin disks encrusted with sesame seeds
Ken, bervakasha
these, please
Shukran
Afwan
I want this
I want Those
2-shekel snakes & ladders game
A bakery in the Old City- The baker spoke to me in Hebrew- Then switched to Arabic when I said "Shukran."
don't buy the pizzas in front
MEYOWWW
Jerusalem
where I buy all my lingerie when I'm in the old city

Thinking of laundry while ordering pizza slices for the kids at Yummy Corner, across the street from the Albright.

school
Kids asking how much
are these horrible snacks
at 7:30 AM

shekel.

little Boys eating
ice cream -
dropping
wrappers on
ground.

Here, try this - sprouted spelt, wheat, rye bread. Try this carob honey & agave sweated orange carob cake. Try this date-stuffed sunflower seed sprouted buckwheat balls - where are you from?

I'm not officially kosher but I've been vegetarian for 30 years!

I wanna try!

I don't need any Rabbi's blessing for that!

You'll like this cake - it isn't so hard as the last time I made it - but still you'd better eat it right away.

How I bought 55 shekels worth of hippie health food junk food.

Helen, look, I'm a little old guy blasting off into space!

Allaah Akbar

Look ma, I'm riding to the moon!

old mop handle

piece of irrigation hose I found in the bushes

Rainy DAY FUN! Feb 1st.

I know you don't like to walk, but it's just a little further and you're just too heavy for me!
Come on! you can do it!
I won't carry you if you just sit there — you have to ask nicely!
Oh, OK, I'll carry you!
Oh, such a heavy pet!

Helen's piece of irrigation hose is so much like her– except in weight!

My pet is so Thirsty!

wow, it really is!

spikey ball

irrigation pipe

again

old mop handle quarterstaff

paper cup full of pine-needles found in the trash.

green lemon stabbed wit a broken CD

"creamsickle"—all the cats are named This. & won't be petted.

surreal toys & pets.

This pizza is yucky.
Excellent Pizza & arak at AZzarah

PHONICS
"Oh Dear," said Moominmama, "what will we have for breakfast now that the kitchen is under water? I do hope I remembered to close the coffee tin lid!"
Mama, what do you do here?
Circle the words that have a short a sound, then write the right word next to the picture.
Is this right?
remember to start your letters at the top.

"I know!" said Moomintroll, "We'll dive for our breakfast!" Moominpapa fetched a saw and began sawing a hole in the floor. "How wonderful to look down on ones own kitchen!" —

what's this page say?

what do you do here?

let's read it: "I Am ——" your choices are Ann, Add, & Bag.

MAAAA-MAAA! Just Read!

Ann - her name is Ann.

OK, write it in the space. You can see how to write it because It's written There. Capital A.

Moomintroll gazed down the hole and watched tea towels drift by like clouds in the summer sky. He took a tremendous breath and dove down into the kitchen.

Does this say Pam?

What do I do here?

you fill in the s if it needs it. "Pam comes — does it need an s?

yes.

fill it in — start at the top

MAAAMAAA! JUST READ!

OK, Helen, enough Phonics for tonight. It's great that you want to work on it - but

PHONICS BOOK is k/i/ck/ed ou/t!

mama, how come there's no one else in costumes?
We're not in the Jewish part of Town. Purim is a Jewish holiday. We'll see kids in costume when we get to Mamilla.
are we jewish?
No, we just look like it today.
CHRISTIAN QUARTER ROAD
Mama, I still don't see any Jews around!
Helen! Don't say that!
Jews = Kids in Costumes

Isn't It great That It's sunny & it isn't raining like It has been for weeks!
yes! It's good Zeus decided to make it sunny for Purim!
The Sun had a lot of dentist appointments, but now it's back.
Helen's theology.
Look! Two Jews!
Helen! You can't say that!
This Country is a Jewish State- but it isn't polite to point like that!
But They must be Jews because They're wearing costumes for Purim!

2nd day of
Swimming Lessons
at The Y.
I'm waiting to see That
T & H will be OK.
Then met the other moms,
who are
Palestinian.
Reem lives
in Biet
Hanina.
The teacher,
Anat
Bashir
age 5. &
Albino
Battle of The big-haired mothers yelling
instructions at Their Kids in the
Childrens' shower
at the Y.
first day of swimming lessons -
March 5

How about you- Do you want anymore children?
No way!
Ha-that's definite!
It's so much work! I have so many other things to do!
And it's expensive!
I know! You know that family in the swimming lessons with all the boys?
They're all the same family?
Yeah.
Yes-their dad is the chef at the cafe- that's how come they can come. Imagine paying for 5! It's bad enough for 2.
Also-how could you pay attention to all those kids? How could you help them all in school? How could you give them what they need?
So do you want to have anymore? Are two boys enough?
This old theme again!
Yes, I want a girl! But my husband says what if it's another boy and we can't afford it!

guys with Coffee
crossing the Seam from
East to West Jerusalem

Return to Us
Return to Us
Return to Us
Boom Boom
Boom Boom
This is BORING! And They're littering!
SSSHHH, Helen! you have to be Quiet during Aphrodite rituals!
Oh, Let her speak her mind! The sound boom isn't connected to the camera!
I paid 12 euros for that basket!
John & Robert finding it difficult.

Oh Aphrodite
Accept our offerings That we return to you in The Sea! We give you these gifts with love!
O Aphrodite! O hear us, Aphrodite! O love us, Aphrodite!
Boom Boom Boom Boom
(What's happening to the basket? Is Aphrodite really going to get it?
What do you think?
No. She said it was gifts- but it's just a bunch of branches, right?
looks like it.
wasn't it wonderful
wonderful, wonderful!
Aphrodite would probably prefer Sticker books anyway!

Well, Kids, How did you like your time in Jerusalem?

Hated it.

We didn't have any toys, You didnt let me bring my giant Callapitter, & The cats didnt let us pet Them!

Oh, Come on! It was fun! Remember Masada & Ein Gedi & all The great felafel?

And you didn't go to school—
wasn't that great?

(I'm still feeling guilty for my failure at home schooling.)

And how about the trips to Cyprus, Lesvos, & Crete?

First day of Winter Vacation

I'm bored.

I'm bored!

I'm bored.

I'm bored!

You're mistaken if you Think That has anyThing to do with me.

I'm bored!

Go out & shovel The drive way.

No.

I'm bored!

Go out & shovel other people's driveways and Then knock on Their doors and ask for money!

No!

I'm bored!

Go out & go up and down The street getting into unspeakable mischief.

No!

I'm bored!

You could go lie down in the middle of The road.

Hehheh. I could try That but,

NO!

I'm bored.

Well, I guess I could read you a book-

OK!

Damn!

P.S. don't miss this chance to spend loving time with son-

Bye! Thanks for having Helen all afternoon!
Sure! Careful on The ice!
mama! You walked?
Of course! It's only 3 blocks.
Did you have fun with C?
You hate me.

What? I love you. Now, why are you saying that?
You took away my toast last night. You hate me.
I took it away because you said it was yucky.
and I'm trying to train you not to say bad Things about your food.
You hate me.
Come, on!
I love you!

LAST NIGHT
Last call for food before bed!
I'll have toast, I guess.
Don't have it if you don't really want it.
I do want it, with lots of butter.
But not toasted too much. Is it the right kind of bread?
This toast is yucky.

No toast for you! Get up to bed!
Hey!
You're so mean & I hate you!
More Than you hate yucky toast?
Mama!

If you say something is yucky, you don't get to eat it too—That's the rule.

You can think yucky Thoughts all you want—Just don't say it. It's too rude.

You're so mean, I can hardly believe how mean you are.

You can say 'no Thanks' but That might not work for something you just requested.

I hate you and you hate me.

I don't hate you! I just want to raise a child who isn't spoiled and rude. I love you!

I love you no matter what.

You hate me.

I love you!

You hate me.

I love you!

you hate me.

I love you!

You sound like a sick elephant.

How was P.E.?

Good. We did The Climbing wall. It's my favorite.

9/8

What would you like for dinner? Macaroni & Cheese?
I guess.

I supose I should offer you a vegetable too. What would you like, a carrot?
I'll have a carrot!
In fact, Helen doesn't need any Vegetables!
We'll eat them for her!

Helen! The Mac 'n' Chee' is ready!
Groan! Do I have to get up?
But I'm not sure it's just how you like it.
stir
sniff
Mmn Turnips in turnip Sauce!
Looks good to me!

I can only eat half. Because the other half is yucky.
May I suggest you make it yourself next time?
I'm too busy.
Are you going to finish That?

Mama! Do my maze!
I will! I just have to take the trash to the curb! Right Now.
MAMA!
Mama! You Ruined EVERYTHING!

I'm sorry! I didn't really wreck it! I followed a path.
You RUINED my maze!
And I've had to take the trash out!
How many times has this happened before?
Maybe you should plow your maze in the front yard instead of the driveway?
NO! This is my maze place!
You use the front yard.
We can't drive around the drive way! & through the front yard!
You RUINED MY MAZE!
Have a swell day at school!
SIGH!

Hi, Helen, how was school?
Fix me a snack.

Tell me specifically what you would like and I'll help you make it.
I guess I won't eat, Then.

I'm saying I'll help you! It's not too hard to slice an apple or some cheese.
You Think I'm old enough to do These Things, but I'm not.

When is old enough to slice cheese? 11? 21? Let me see your cheese-slicing license! Sorry: Too young!
Mama! You're not taking This seriously!

Watch out-
here comes a
car.
OK, but I'm
Not holding
your hand.
Because if I do it would
look like we're a happy
family.
And we're
NOT!

Why do you have to hold his hand? Now There's no room for me!
I have This other hand especially designed for you!
No offence, but it's poisoned.
By The fact That your brother is on The other side?
You can't love us both! He has to go.
We've made it This far together- let's let him stay.
I knew it! You love him more!

Look at That cute dog!
Oh look - There's another cute dog!
Or maybe...
It's The same dog, but in two different panels.
This kid reads a lot of comics.

"Charles Wallace walked purposefully ahead of them—" Helen! What are you doing?
No lick! Roll that tongue right back in & keep it there!
meyow?
Keep reading!
Hey!
Don't put your nose on me!
Why not? It's what I do!
Your nose is always cold! Here, I'll warm it up for you!
yuck!
Keep Reading!

10/4

Mama,
If I could have one wish.

It would be to live in Lulu & Tubby & Nancy & Sluggo times.

What? Even though legos had not been invented yet?

Yes - it would be worth it to go back there with all I know from reading all the comics...

And get back at those girls for once!

Why doesn't any thing exciting ever happen?
On our way to CAPE COD (Grandma's house) for WINTER BREAK.
What do you mean by exciting?
Oh, my birthday with a bouncy castle with a slide into a pool.

Or a water park! Can't we go to a water park?
I've never been to a water park!
Actually we went to That one....
Oh yeah!
But There were so many rules!

No standing on The divider between pools, no jumping off The divider. Very strict!

No running, no food, no teenagers making out behind The waterfall!
Disgusting wet bathrooms with clogged toilets, soggy hot dogs,
Not enough naked girls in The changing room!
And we had to leave almost right after we got There!

We're not even going There and already There is so much wrong with it!

Can't we please go to a waterpark?

Next Stop: Malcontenta, waterpark!

When are we going to get There?

This Summer visit
AQUALITT
Splash-tastic fun for the whole family!
Endless Euro-culture entertainment!
EUROPE'S ONLY LITERARY - THEMED WATER PARK
Why do we have to be here?
We promised your sister a break from museums.
Whee!
No, I mean in general.
Where to first?
Daddy! Put that away and go on a slide!
In Search of Lost Time
Why does everthing have to have a theme? Isn't shooting down a plain plastic tube full of water fun enough?
JUDE the OBSCURE
AQUALITT
Where's the tallest slide with the shortest line?

ODYSSEY
How was the slide?
Really fun!
Though they made us wear these foam heads, so we couldn't really see where we were going.
Where's Daddy?
Oink! Oink!
DANTE'S DIVINE COMEDY
The spiral chute into the pit of Hell was awesome!
Lucky! I was stuck on the Purgatory slide with all these slow people meandering around until we got dumped out into a swamp.
Next time you have to choose Hell.
JULIUS CAESAR
Don't freak! It washes off.
Hey Mama, "Et tu, Brute?" Haha!
POKE POKE

MADAME BOVARY
I feel Kind of sick! I'm hungry for something not arsenic-y.
Gosh, the crushing ennui of existence! All the twists and turns and chutes of life add up to what, anyway?
Can we get ice cream?
THE CASTLE
GULAG ARCHIPELAGO
That one took a while!
We waited in line and when we got to the front they wouldn't let us in and said we had to get permission and to wait in this other line and we did, since we didn't want to lose our places, but then...
...somehow we ended up on this other side, and, frankly we're lucky to be alive.
Ow, ow, frostbite!
Wuthering Heights
Wasn't it so awesome how you had to bash the side out of Cathy's Coffin to get out of the slide?
Yeah, and to get on the Slide you had to break that window pane and scream, "Let me in!"
And how the wind whistled across the Moors! In the Slide!
Not even death can separate us from this slide.

NO EXIT
There you are!
I can't believe they made us go on a raft with two complete strangers!
Hell is other people. Can we leave now?
Daddy's bac One more slid Daddy?

But even if someone a million years from now found This cup—They'd never know how good This foamy milk chai is now.

True.

Mama, It's cold out-
You should wear a hat.
Actually it's not that cold - I don't need one.
Yes, you do!
Here wear This.
See it IS cold! I'd hate to have you catch a chill and come down with a nasty head cold!
What a kind caring daughter!
Mama! Don't take The hat off in The store! The main purpose is to prevent your hair from looking all grizzled! And it does!

Well, what are the bunnies doing today?
"Today we're having a giant snow ball battle to the death!"

No, the bunnies are not doing that!
"Why not? We love pelting each other with snow!"

Because, as you know, It's Spring in Bunny World - There's no snow!
"But we're here with you! Not in Bunny World!"
"Watch out here comes a snowball!"
punch
"And another! And Another!"
Mama! The bunnies can't throw snowballs! Their aim isn't that good!

The bunnies are not having a snowball fight!
"But Helen, we want to! We love playing in the snow!"
It's spring- There is no snow.
"This sure looks like snow to me!"
Nope. Not allowed.
"Whaaah!" "We want to play in the snow!"
Quit, Bunny.
"Let us play! We already built this big ole igloo!"
No, they didn't.
Well, if you think about it there are no bunnies or Bunny world so it doesn't matter whether it's snowing or not.
The bunnies are getting ready for the Spring Garden Party and scavenger hunt. The sun is shining and there's a warm breeze. Think of a clue:

Mama, who is Ronald Regan?
He was president when I was in high School and a Republican so not good as well as Kind of ridiculous.
BOR-ING!
Hey! You asked! You can't ask me a question and Then say "BORING" IT'S SO RUDE!
Why do you always misinterpret what I'm saying? I didn't mean it like That!
It sure sounded completely rude and bratty!
It's like you're thinking the wrong Thing about me on purpose! To make me feel bad!
Just don't say "Boring" when someone answers a question!
Especially about Political History.

Why do you wear bell-bottoms ?
They aren't that bell-y. They're good pants- they fit and all.
Mama, The thing you have to do is look at what other people are wearing and wear stuff like that.
How do you do that and keep a sense of your unique self at the same time?
Don't even worry about it.

Mama, you can't wear that coat.
Why not?
Oh.
Not that coat either – It's too much like my coat.
I can't wear my winter coat in case you wear your winter coat at the same time? How did we end up with the same coat?
You're changing coats? That one's from last year. Does it still fit? Is it warm enough?
It's fine!
Now you can wear your coat.
No, it's too heavy for today. I'll go change my pants so I can wear my other coat.
What about that hat?

What? What's wrong with the hat?
Its tallness increases your nose-length, is all.
What if I pull it down really far and try to make the pompom go straight back?
UGh.
Any way, This is the only hat I've got.
You should buy another hat.
SPROING!
Hey, you have these same gloves, too?
They're both mine. I bought another pair because you took the first pair and lost them.
I didn't lose them, I'm wearing them.
Wait! Is it O.K. that we're wearing the same gloves?
I'll Keep my hands in my pockets.
Mama, This hat is definitely the wrong shape for your head.
How do you Know it's not the look I'm going for?
If it is, you shouldn't.

It's freezing! Let's hop!
Hippity hop!
Hippity hop! Hippity hop! Hippity hippity hop hop hop!
Mama! Stop!
Hippity hop!
You're a public nuisance!
Hello.
'Lo
UGh.
Don't use our time chatting!
You don't think it would be way *hipper* if we were wearing identical coats?
"Hippen"? Really, Mama? Really?
Get that big nose off me!

How about this one?
No! No Way!
Same problem as The hat you already have.
This one? I kind of like This one. But it's expensive.
Hmm.
It's O.K. Kind of pumpkin-y.
How about this one for me?
Very cute.
But you already have ten hats and definitely don't need another one.
How about this one?
Not your style.
I have a style?
Let's get out of here.
Wait, you're not buying even one hat?
None of them were improve-ments on The dumb hat I already have.
Still, if you bought one, then you'd have TWO dumb hats!
Hey, how about we trade? You wear this hat That will look good on you no matter what, and I'll wear your cute hat.
Ha ha, Mama, you're out of your mind.

NOTHING TO WEAR

A CATALOG OF CLOTHES AND WHY I CAN'T WEAR ANY OF THEM.

Unacceptable SHORTS

SOFT COTTON SHORTS. Weird Color: Kakhi. NOT A COLOR. THESE DO NOT GO with any Thing. Also They are far too long.

SAME COTTON SHORTS, but in pool blue. Too many blue shirts make These impossible to wear. BLUE + BLUE = NOT ALLOWED. ALSO: TOO LONG.

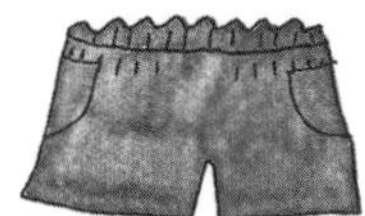

COTTON TWILL SHORTS WITH A GATHERED WAIST. All poochy in back. Are you Crazy? NOT OK.

SHORTS WITH WATERMELONS ALL OVER THEM. Technically These are good, but not today because we're probably having watermelon at camp and That would look planned/redundant/ironic and someone might notice and comment.

JEANS SHORTS HANDED DOWN FROM SEXY COUSI Weird lines around Crotch. Too short.

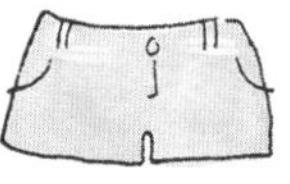

COTTON TWILL SHORTS in lilac. These might be OK if not lilac Lilac is too girly a color.

PLAIN NON-DESCRIPT SHORTS in Stone THAT I <u>could</u> wear and you wouldn't even notice. I don't feel like wearing these today. Or ever.

BLACK RUNNING SHORTS. These are The best and I would wear Them every day but They must be reserved for Special Occasions - i.e. not today because Then They might be in The laundry in case I need Them tomorrow or The next day.

JEANS SHORTS WITH LACE ON THE LEGS. JUST KIDDING. I DON'T OWN THESE! IF I DID, I'D ALREADY BE DEAD BY NOW.

SHIRTS THAT I CAN'T WEAR, ALTHOUGH SOMETIMES I'M DRIVEN TO BY DIRE CIRCUMSTANCES.

GREEK SOCCER SHIRT. I'm not interested in soccer but like the bright lime green color. Stains on front don't matter in this case. Have to fold collar under, otherwise it looks weird.

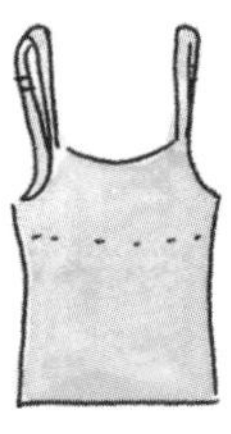

TANK-TOP, POOL BLUE. Do I detect a shelf-bra? Eeyew! NO WAY WILL THE SUMMER EVER BE HOT ENOUGH for me to wear this.

BUGS BUNNY SHIRT No one knows who Bugs Bunny is so I can't wear this. People would ask questions.

TIE-DYED BEN & JERRY'S SHIRT. This is my favorite and so either I'm wearing it or it's in the laundry, in which case I must wail and groan.

STRIPED SHIRT FROM OLD NAVY. This looks so normal, like something a normal kid would wear, so that, well, sorry.

PLAIN SPORTY SHIRT. It's like the soccer shirt but without the decoration or the limey color. This shirt is so dull that it's intollerable to look at, let alone wear.

Mama, I have no clothes. Aren't you going to do anything about it?

Cypro archaic I
Museum July 13

Hey Kiddo! I'm glad you found a book you really like!
I got a few more from the library.

You've been reading non-stop. It looks like you're almost finished with that book—
and we still have another week of vacation!

The librarian recommended a bunch of new books: If you liked the Dark Cities books, here's another by the same author.
GLOOM TOWN

And she said if you're into the Elemental Magicians cycle, to check out the latest...
Enchanted Helium

And I got a couple of books in the Apprentice Mage series— I know you liked those. Does it matter if you read them in order?
BOOK 22
MAGE'S BOOK OF BLOOD
BOOK 13
FALSE APPRENTICE

It might have for the first five — that's as far as I've read — but then I realized those books have too many words.

"Hükk shook the sweat out of his eyes as he lunged at his enemy, and with a series of deft strokes with his flashing blade, every movement a testament to his years of training, he forced his enemy to step backwards, causing him to lose his footing on the crumbling shale at the edge of the precipice. Hükk shrugged as his enemy plunged headlong into the yawning maw of the chasm."

I guess the first few books were pretty exciting— there was the exiled princess in disguise and the main hero who forced the volcano to erupt with his mind in order to swamp the zombie pig wolf invasion in lava.

But by the fifth book, you knew none of the main characters would die, and they ran out of things to do, so they just meandered around, rescuing trolls who fell down wells, and that doesn't constitute a plot.

I think they keep fighting Count Darkness and his Minyans, but even if he gets ahold of the sword of Snërg, ensuring ultimate victory, I don't think I can make it through all those words to find out for sure.

So I guess that's a NO to Children of Darkness: Apprentices of Light? Or Mage Ghosted?
I suspect that author is just writing for the money.
BOOK 24 THE MAGE WHO GOT PAID

Why not try another that's not in that series?
They all look like depressing imitations of The Lord of the Rings.
It's rough for the poor writers of today!

But who knows, you might get into one of these books, like you have with the book you're reading now! Why not read all the first chapters and see what you think?

Look, this chapter is like a hundred pages long! It's thicker than an Ipad! It obviously has too much of something if it thinks it can be this long!

There are too many characters named with too many vowels, and too many descriptions of impassable swamps! How is this relevant to anything?
Oh heck, Princess Ayaiyaië, we're lost!
The Goddess Oïa is supposed to help our Quest!
By Great Owywiewi's beard, we're doomed!
Chin up! There's Castle Eyrwyn right over there!
But it looks haunted!

Besides, the more you read, the longer the book gets. Actually, it mutates, wraps around your body, and devours you like a boa constrictor.
Help! I'm only on page twelve!
01

OK, OK, why not just try reading the first page of each book? That can't kill you.

And then no one could say you judged a book by its dark-sword-dragon-quest cover.
Airship Kingdom!
WRAITH ACADEMY
INSUBSTANTIAL BUT SPIRITED!
DRAGON SNARL
BOOK 5 • DRAGON EXHALE SERIES
SWORD of GLOAMING
NOT VERY BRIGHT DOESN'T MEAN IT ISN'T DEADLY!
DARK DREAMS
BATTLE of the HEDGE MAGES
DUST QUEST
CITY OF GUM.

I'm already reading this book. I don't need another one.

Maybe you're tired of fantasy? I've also got this other one— it's about some kids in school.
Anyway, So There!

Not that book! We had to read that in school. We're always reading books about kids who learn to accept things-like death—
Anyway, So There!

or other people they thought they hated because they're different, or worse, they learn to accept themselves for who they are!
Sigh!
Now go away, I'm reading!

The dwarfs have a king?
I thought dwarfs were
too short to be kings.

There's nothing very
interesting about that
pig. It's just a pig.
And the book isn't even
really about the pig.

If the food at that school
is so bad, why didn't Jane
just bring her own lunch?

I don't want to hear about any more girls who are mamas getting turned into cows or shrubs or anything else.

She gets an orange for Christmas and that's *it*? I'd be so MAD.

This guy has a talking bird? No fair. Can we get a talking bird? I'd take care of it.

That supper at the end— What if I don't like it? Could I have something else?

again.

Why are they having Seed cake? Why can't they have regular cake with frosting? Why have cake, anyway, was it some Hobbit's birthday?

That farm girl Lucy who saved Hazel— she doesn't deserve to have rabbits. Also— can we get some? I'll take care of them and make sure they don't fight.

Why would that kid want to kiss Estella? Eeeyew! She's probably actually really ugly.

What's "aggravate" mean? What's "negligence"? What's "morose"? What's "impertinence"? What's "grotesque"? I don't care that we're only on page 2 — don't keep reading this book!

Heathcliff! It's me, Cathy! And a whole lot of vocabulary words!

Today I'm taking Charlotte Brontë to yoga.
Sangha Studio
What's yoga?

It's exercise, but also a bit like church.
I won't have to speak to anyone, will I?
Propably not.

Hi Keighley, this is Charlotte. I'll pay for her.
First time here, Charlotte? Welcome.

Keighley is the name of the town from where I sent my manuscript of Jane Eyre.
I Know! Quite a coincidence!
It's not a girl's name, though.
It is now.

Here's your mat.
I'll just sit here out of the way and do some sewing.
The mat is here in case you change your mind.

Wait! Should we be here?

There are men here!
And women in their underwear!
It's yoga-wear! Don't worry, everyone stays on his or her own mat.
They aren't driven to embrace right here?
If they are, they wait until after class.
Then must they marry? And won't many children result?
Not as many as you might think— because of Birth Control.
This changes the moral fabric of society completely.
And probably allows us to be in the same room together.
We also have antibiotics— so no more TB.
Good morning! How's everyone feeling today?

Start seated at the end of your mat. Take a moment to set aside the events of your day and begin to bring your awareness to your breath.... Now begin to deepen your breath... Even inhales and exhales....
Isn't it rude to breathe so much among men?
Let the breath lead the way to awareness of your inner landscape and your true self....
Does she really think this is possible without a pen in one's hand?
Where's that eerie music coming from?
Sound system. It's normal.
....move into down-ward facing dog.
Everyone has their nether-end in the air! In public!
Charlotte! Settle down! Why not try it?
No one will look at you. They're all too busy with their own practice.
I'm looking at them.
I am too, actually. It's interesting to see people's bums. But don't be distracted! Try it!
My clothes aren't very stretchy. I'm afraid I'll pop my seams.
And then I'll have to spend time repairing them when I could be writing.
Take off a layer!
I thought I was fit — you know how I walk miles on the moors every day! But my arm-strength seems to lie mostly in holding a quill.

Remember you can always drop your Knees in Chataranga... This is your practice.
Especially yours, Charlotte Brontë.
Oof.
Forty five minutes later...
Take any final movements before settling in to shavasana.
What's happening now?
Now we lie here for five minutes with our eyes closed.
Use this time to absorb all the good things you've gained from practice today.
I'll just get my sewing.
No, stay here! This part is part of it!
Oh, is this when men and women embrace when no one can see?
No, not even now.
We finish class with the sound of OM.
OM
What's this for?
Does that man over there look like Napoleon to you?
After Class...
You're Charlotte Brontë? I had to read Jane Eyre in school. It was good, though.
It's cool you do yoga.
Catch you later.

We weren't even introduced! Do men bother you?
Once one sweated on me— but then he apologized.
A gentleman, then! But these men are all covered in tattoos, like pirates!
The women too! How is it allowed?
It's a fashion.
Then I want no part of it!
And—
Women make their own decisions about tattoos and most other things as well.
If I did get one, I'd have a full-length Mr. Rochester right here.
Or maybe the names of Emily and Anne inscribed within the feather of a quill pen.
Why not both?
Do women publish under their own names without fear of being judged by their sex?
Mostly!
And are women paid the same for their novels?
Practically! There are laws, anyway.
What wondrous times these are.
Things are far from perfect.
I go to Keighley's class to keep from getting too gloomy.
What possible reason could you have for feeling gloomy?
I'll bet Mr. Rochester would benefit by this yoga class.
Good luck getting him to come.

Nicosia garden

APRIL VACATION
Mama! Come downstairs!
I will! I just have to finish something!
Mama, are you coming?
Yes! Right away!
Mama, I'm going to cry if you don't come now.
Just hang on! I'll be right There!
OK, Helen, I'm here now. What did you want?
It's too Late! I don't know any more!

Mama, will you draw with me?
Sure - but I have a few Things I have to get done first.
I knew you'd say no.
I'm NOT saying no! I just have to brush my teeth, Start The laundry and The dish-washer.
That'll take forever.
You're telling me.
Mama! If you don't get down here I'm going to start crying again!
I'm COMING!
Mama, it's clear That you don't want to draw with me.
Helen, it's clear you don't know about all The stuff I have to do to keep This place going!
Have you brushed your teeth yet?

Helen, daddy has to go to Cyprus for 2 months. You and me and Sylvan are going for one month-
Don't you think it's better for us to go than to be apart for so long?
I guess. I hope it's not going to be like Greece.
It's not. at all.
When are we going?
JULY.
Noooo! I want to be here for my birthday!
What if they don't have cake there?
My whole birthday will be RUINED if it's in some Greek place!
We'll make it good. We could go to a water park.
Waterpark?
Want to see some pictures?
yes.
There are three! Hey look at this one - it's the closest. It has an Ancient Greek Theme.
Ruined! It's all ruined!

IN MY STUDIO, ABOUT TO MAKE ONE MARK ON PAPER, AFTER DOING LAUNDRY & DISHES.

MAMA!

You're probably hungry. Baguette with cheese? Toast? Can of soup? Mac 'n' Chee?

OK

Helen has been drawing all morning. The minute I tried to work she called me.

Where are you going?

Upstairs for a minute.

No!

Mama...
You annoy me.
I'm sure I do.
Take a break from me! Go someplace else! Go to your own room!
Noooo!
Mama, you're trying to get rid of me!
No, only trying to get out of range of being annoying!

Stop staring at Me!

I can't help it! You look so extra-ordinary with your hair up like That.
STOP.

I'm staring at you here & here & here & here.
Mama! Stop!
POKE
POKE

MY BODY AND MY DAUGHTER

AN IN-DEPTH ANALYSIS *by* GLYNNIS FAWKES

But you can see your boob crack!
Is that bad?
What's wrong with boobs?
After all, I fed you from them for a year.

squeeze
palpate
No! Don't flex your muscle!
I like it better when it's all squishy and wobbly.

Ugg.
There they are again.
What? My boobs?
Mama, I can't believe you boob-mooned us!

Mama, I'll show you a neat trick.
Look, now your skin is all wrinkly like an old elephant trunk.
Can you do it on yourself?
No, it's no fun, It doesn't work.

squeeze
squeeze
Get away from me with those little Kneading Kitten paws!
But your belly is so squishy and pooodgy!
No! Get off!
Poodge, Poodge,
Squish, squish!

What's this?
Oh, just something growing there, a mole.
It's horrible. You should cut it off!

I just pulled off a blood blister scab from when I stubbed my toe.
Eeyew!
Why tell me? TMI!
I thought you'd be interested.

Goodnight, Helen!
Why did you have to name me that?
It's a beautiful name!
My grandmother was Helen.
She was elegant. Long before I was born, or even my mother was born, my grandfather used to say:
Oh Hell-
Oh Hell
Oh Helen!
Oh Lige!

Isn't HELL a bad word? I don't want a swear word in my name!

Hell, no, it isn't a swear word, it's an interesting place. You go to heaven for the climate and to hell for the company.

There's also Mt. St. Helens:

You named me after a volcano?

And of course there's Helen of Troy-

the most beautiful woman—

That's bad— because I'm not.

Remember how that Helen was born?

But I'm not beautiful.
You don't need to think you are— but you are.
"I have a little girl: the golden flowers are no match for her loveliness."
Mama, that's dumb!
No, it's Sappho! "I would not trade her for all the gold..."
Mama, quit.
So we're not going to Troy after all?
No, we've been re-routed to Vermont.
And not to do battle—
but to deliver treats to a lovely 8-year-old-
Helen-
The holds are loaded...
...with waffles and syrup, drawing pads, pens, and chalk.
Hey! Are you ship #1001?
Yes. I'm here to record the story!
Glynnis Fawkes 2015

FIRST DAY OF SUMMER VACATION

Whee! New hammock!
Mama, how does it work?

That Kid Freddy in my class? He's my enemy!

Why? What did he do?
Nothing!
I just have to chase him around a lot during recess because he's my enemy!

Is it because he's also good at drawing and you're jealous?
No! He's just my enemy! And I don't want him to be in the same summer camp because he'll see me in my bathing suit!

That's 6 months away! Don't worry about it!
I don't want that enemy staring at me in my bathing suit! Because that's what he'll do!

what's wrong with him seeing you in your bathing suit?
Daddeee! Duh! My bathing suit just barely covers my privates!
And besides- my bathing suits are all pink & green & colors like That!
But They do cover your privates.
which is The main job of a bathing suit.
He'll still be staring at me. He'll see The shape of everyThing!
Stare right back!
Don't want to! He's my enemy!

The kids have spent an hour on the time-honored sport of defacing newspapers with moustaches and wienies. They were laughing their heads off. But now look at the place.
KIDS! Get in here and stack these papers neatly!
And now set the table, please!
Mama doesn't love Helen.
Mama treats Helen as a common servant.
No love, just chores & more chores.
Mama won't play with Helen. It's just work, work, work all the time.
All because Mama doesn't love poor Helen.

How're those cookies, good?
No Duh!

"No Duh"! Listen to you! Is that what kids at school say?
No Duh!

Just don't say "No Duh" to grandma when we go to visit.
No Duh!

Even if she asks whether I like the present she gets me?
Duh, No!

FLOW CHART OF AIR TRAVEL ANXETIES
GETTING TO THE AIRPORT
UBER/LYFT/TAXI NEVER ARRIVES. I STAY HOME.
YAWN
Visit Europe
IT ARRIVES, BUT THE DRIVER GIVES ME A RARE NEAR-FATAL VIRUS.
COUGH Have a safe trip. COUGH
IT ARRIVES, BUT THE DRIVER GETS LOST AND TAKES TWO HOURS TO FIND THE AIRPORT AND CHARGES ACCORDINGLY.
That will be $395, please
AIRPORT CHECK-IN
KIOSK HAS NO RECORD OF MY RESERVATION.
I ONLY DREAMED I BOUGHT TICKETS.
FLIGHTS.COM
COMPLETE PURCHASE
CLICK!
ZZZZ
I BOUGHT THE TICKETS, BUT FOR SOME FUTURE DATE.
This reservation is for 2028.
SECURITY
FAMILIAR OBJECTS TURN OUT TO BE MADE OF ILLEGAL SUBSTANCES.
What is this?
My eraser brush!! I need it for my work.
Full of uranium.
MY NEW PANTS SET OFF THE METAL DETECTOR.
I'm sorry, Ma'am. We're going to have to search the area.
BEEP BEEP BEEP
NEW SECURITY REGULATIONS
SECURITY DELAYED FOR TWO HOURS, I MISS THE FLIGHT.
The TSA no longer allows ball-point pens, gum, or socks on all flights.
Your mindless participation keeps our skies super-safe!

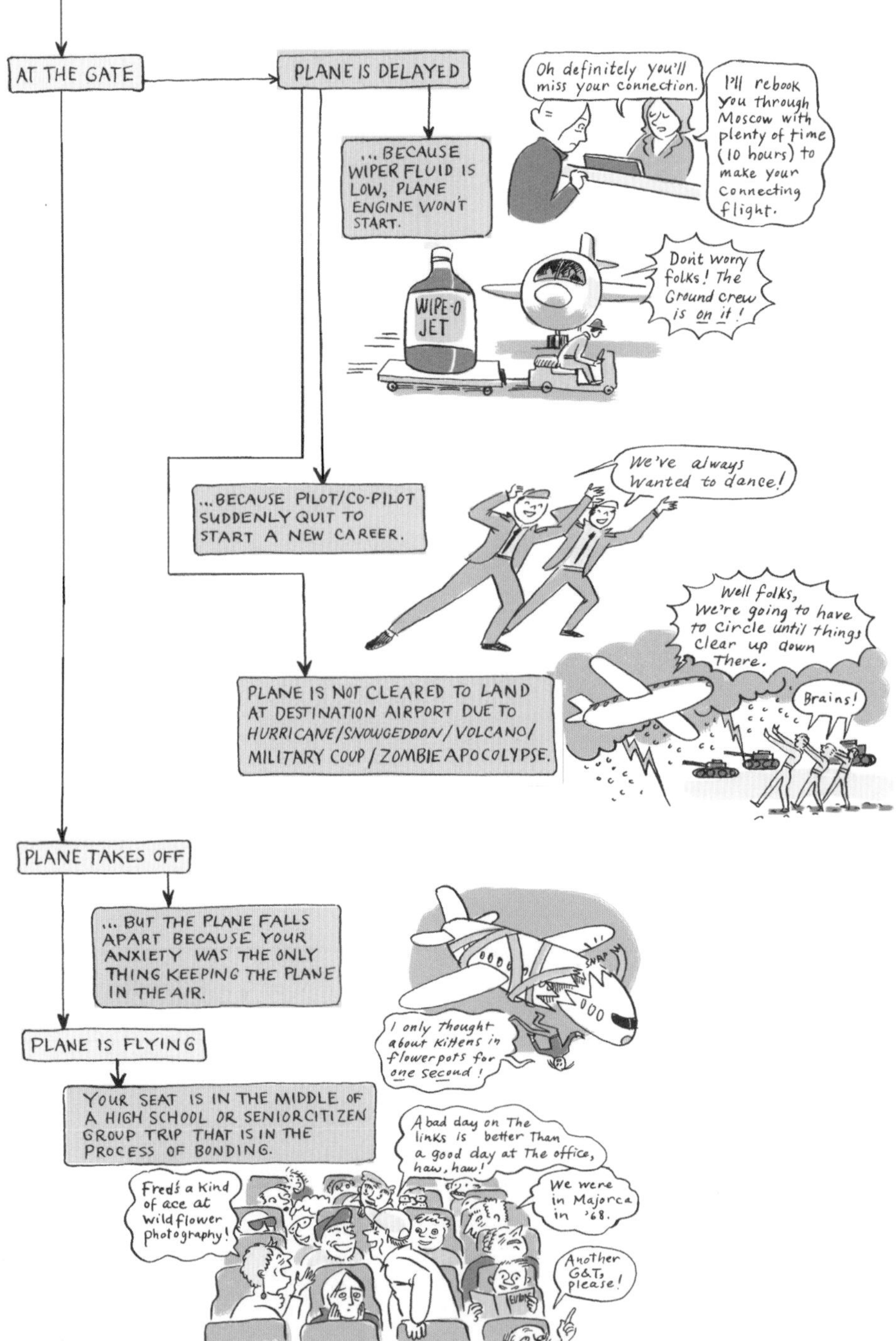
AT THE GATE
PLANE IS DELAYED
Oh definitely you'll miss your connection.
I'll rebook you through Moscow with plenty of time (10 hours) to make your connecting flight.
... BECAUSE WIPER FLUID IS LOW, PLANE ENGINE WON'T START.
WIPE-O JET
Don't worry folks! The Ground crew is on it!
... BECAUSE PILOT/CO-PILOT SUDDENLY QUIT TO START A NEW CAREER.
We've always wanted to dance!
Well folks, We're going to have to circle until things clear up down There.
Brains!
PLANE IS NOT CLEARED TO LAND AT DESTINATION AIRPORT DUE TO HURRICANE/SNOWGEDDON/VOLCANO/MILITARY COUP/ZOMBIE APOCOLYPSE.
PLANE TAKES OFF
... BUT THE PLANE FALLS APART BECAUSE YOUR ANXIETY WAS THE ONLY THING KEEPING THE PLANE IN THE AIR.
SNAP
I only thought about kittens in flowerpots for one second!
PLANE IS FLYING
YOUR SEAT IS IN THE MIDDLE OF A HIGH SCHOOL OR SENIOR CITIZEN GROUP TRIP THAT IS IN THE PROCESS OF BONDING.
Fred's a kind of ace at wildflower photography!
A bad day on The links is better Than a good day at The office, haw, haw!
We were in Majorca in '68.
Another G&T, please!

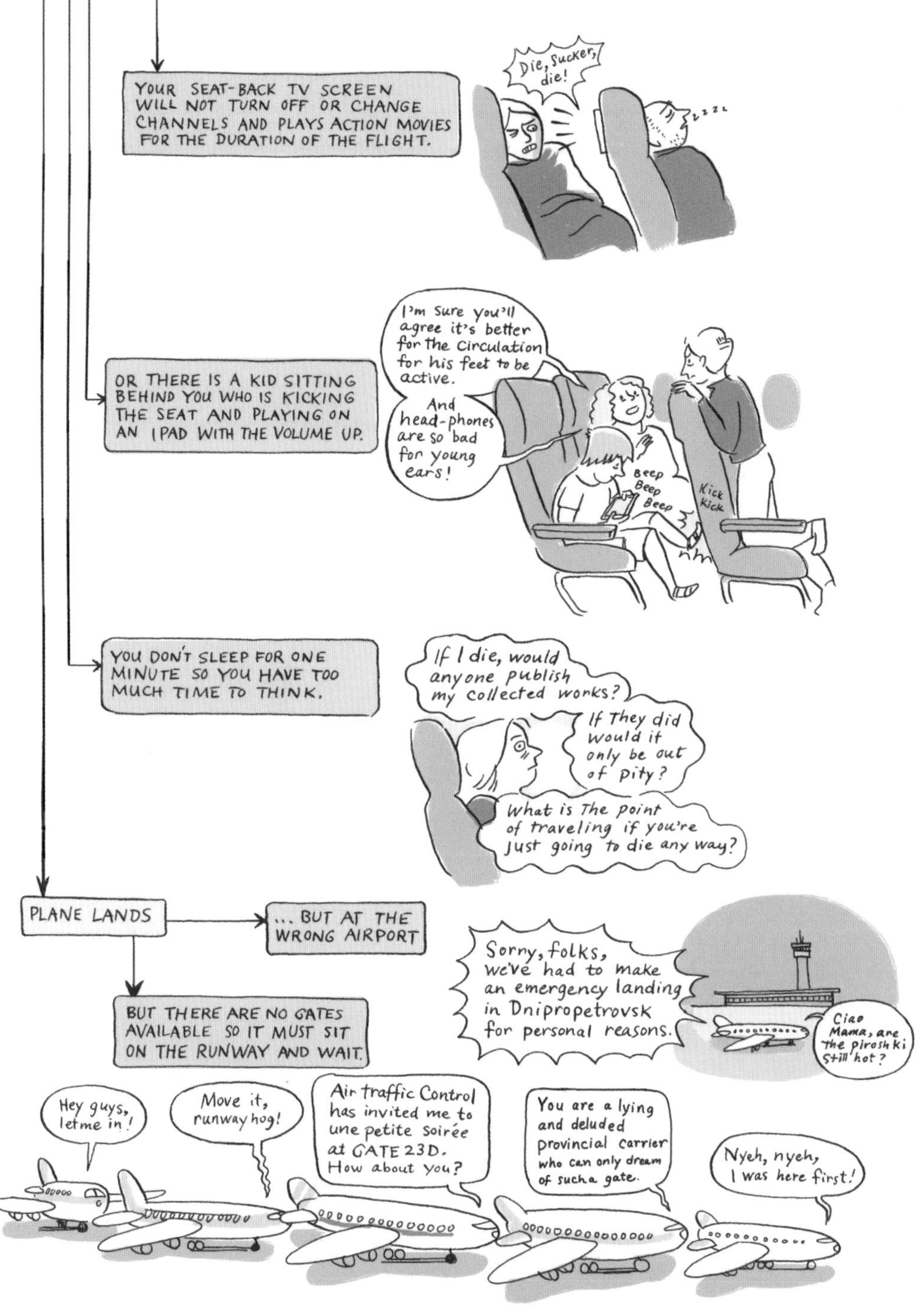
YOUR SEAT-BACK TV SCREEN WILL NOT TURN OFF OR CHANGE CHANNELS AND PLAYS ACTION MOVIES FOR THE DURATION OF THE FLIGHT.
Die, sucker, die!
zzzz
OR THERE IS A KID SITTING BEHIND YOU WHO IS KICKING THE SEAT AND PLAYING ON AN IPAD WITH THE VOLUME UP.
I'm sure you'll agree it's better for the circulation for his feet to be active.
And head-phones are so bad for young ears!
Beep Beep Beep
Kick Kick
YOU DON'T SLEEP FOR ONE MINUTE SO YOU HAVE TOO MUCH TIME TO THINK.
If I die, would anyone publish my collected works?
If they did would it only be out of pity?
What is the point of traveling if you're just going to die any way?
PLANE LANDS
... BUT AT THE WRONG AIRPORT
Sorry, folks, we've had to make an emergency landing in Dnipropetrovsk for personal reasons.
Ciao Mama, are the piroshki still hot?
BUT THERE ARE NO GATES AVAILABLE SO IT MUST SIT ON THE RUNWAY AND WAIT.
Hey guys, letme in!
Move it, runway hog!
Air traffic Control has invited me to une petite soirée at GATE 23D. How about you?
You are a lying and deluded provincial carrier who can only dream of such a gate.
Nyeh, nyeh, I was here first!

EXIT TO PASSPORT CONTROL
NO EXIT. YOU ARE HELD FOR REASONS BEYOND YOUR CONTROL.
Your country of origin is no longer on speaking terms with this country. You haven't been on twitter in the last six hours, I guess?
OFFICIAL ASKS A LOT OF PERSONAL QUESTIONS, THEN GIVES YOU HIS NUMBER AND OFFERS TO "SHOW YOU AROUND" HIS BEAUTIFUL COUNTRY.
You're American, you say? Do you have a bank account?
You are even more beautiful than you are in the photo that was taken when you were younger, am I right?
NEARLY ETERNAL LINE
YOU MISS YOUR CONNECTING FLIGHT
You should have waited in that line a little more quickly.
We can rebook you Through Kiev with a 12-hour lay-over.
EXISTENTIAL THOUGHTS
Who among these masses cares at all for the expressive power of comics?
EXIT TO GROUND TRANSPORTATION
RETURN TO START...
At least I'm in Europe!
cough cough

AMERICAN KIDS ABROAD

Wait! Daddy, will it be plain? Will there be stuff on it?
We'll see, won't we.

Where's my fooood? I'm starving!
Don't eat any more bread. I'm sure it will come soon.

HALF AN HOUR LATER...
Here you are...
Thank you!
Where's mine?

... and for you,
my dear.
Yum.

It has
flecks.

Daddy, can
you eat it?
Meyow!

Here, I'll cut it up for you.
I'm full.
Oh look! So cute!
Meyoooo!

Here you go— give it a try.

It has cheese inside?
Cheese!!
Meyow.

We didn't know!
Even we can't predict a sneak-attack of cheese stuffing.
So cute!
I'm dying!
meyow.
Can I feed it to the kitty?

Not at the table. We'll ask for a to-go box.
Meyow!
meyoow.

Can we leave?
Soon as we pay.
Ice Cream?
Clap Clap Clap
crunch munch

Hey Kids! Today we're going to a museum.
I'll stay here.
Why do you hate us so much?
Come on! It will be fun. We won't stay long.
Any time in a museum is too long.
You know we hate museums. Why do you have to torture us?
Maybe, once you look around, you'll realize it's interesting.
I'm not looking around.
I'm not coming.
I made them walk around before I gave them the Ipad.

Next we're stopping at a small castle.
You promised no more old stuff!
We didn't.
I'm not getting out of the car.
In five minutes it will be two hundred and fifty degrees in there.
Can't you imagine ancient pirate ships out there?
O.K., we get it. Let's go
Don't lean too far, dear.
Can we please go back to the Airbnb now?
Yes, but listen, kids! We're not trying to kill you on this vacation! We're trying to share the experience of seeing amazing places together!
Mama put me in graveyard. Mama dance on grave. Mama laugh.

Today we thought we'd give you kids a break and go to the beach.
Not going.
It's supposed to be very beautiful...
I'm tired of you dragging us somewhere every day without ever asking if we want to go!
I never wanted to come on this trip at all so I'm staying here.
We'd better leave now_ your brother's been by himself at the hotel all day.
It's no fair that he ruins all the fun!

In July 2017 I visited Cyprus with my family. One morning I took a walk with my daughter through Nicosia.
Let's cross over to The North side.
Can we get ice cream?
ΗΡΑΚΛΗΣ
ICE-CREAM
ΜΠΑΡ
Later – after we cross.
Why do we need passports here?
We're crossing the border.
What border?
Efkharisto.
THREE MINUTES AND EIGHTY METERS LATER...
You have to show them again?
That was the Greek side. This is The Turkish side.
POLIS
PASAPORT KONTROL
Teşekkürler.
Now we're in Northern Cyprus.
I thought we were in Nicosia.
We are – but also in a different Country.
EFES
Why did we come here?

Because— I'm curious.
When I lived here from 1999-2003 - before you were born— The border was only open to foreigners.
Selimiye Mosque- formerly Agia Sophia Cathedral
The archaeologists I worked for considered crossing to The North to be supporting the illegal occupation. So I didn't.
Also— It didn't seem fair that I should go as a tourist to places Cypriots Couldn't.
NICOSIA WALLED CITY
So, like every-one else, I got used to living in half a city.
See how the walls are a perfect Circle?
They were built by The Venetians in the 1500s.
My friend Ruth remembers cycling the circuit of the ramparts after school— it must have been The late 1950s. It her took forty-eight minutes.
In 1964, trouble between Greek and Turkish communities caused The British Peace-Keepers to create a de-militarized buffer zone— The Green Line.
In the summer of 1974 the Turkish army invaded. Greek Cypriots living in the northern third of the island had to evacuate— same with the Turkish Cypriots in the South.
About 6,000 Greek Cypriots and 1500-3500 Turkish Cypriots were Killed, and many were missing. Many also lost property, farmland, and livlihoods.

This place is sketchy.
Well, it's poor.
The only country that recognizes the North is Turkey—so there isn't much outside help.
The Greek side has EU funding—as well as private investors—but that doesn't always go well—the banks crashed in 2012.
Zahra Bastion
Can we go back now?
Since 2003—just after I left—the border opened for Cypriots and they could finally see the places they or their parents came from.
LOZAN SOKAK
But imagine coming back to your house after 30 years to find another family living there!
I'd kick 'em out!
Then where would that family live? It can never be like it was before.
Some people are fighting in court for their lost property.
But I don't know how they'll ever resolve it.
Finally, ice cream!
But I don't have any Turkish lire! So we'd better go back across.
EFES
EFES Pilsen

I visited my parents in August 2017. My mother liked to be in the garden.
She designed this garden and planted everything. When we moved in (when I was seven) the yard was an empty patch of weedy grass.
She snips off dry leaves that will fall anyway.
Hi, Ma, I'm here to help.
She carries a few at a time to the yard debris bin.
Oh, good.
Lately the weeds have returned.
See these? These are no good.
Yeah, those have to go.

There's a lot of bind-weed in the rosemary. I think if I pull it out it will just grow back.
You probably have to dig it up. Things grow like crazy here.
Where do you live?
By now this question shouldn't startle me— she's had Alzheimer's for a few years now, but before that, she visited our house twice a year for the past ten years.
In Vermont— on the other side of the country.
Oh. Do you like it?
Well, we moved there because of John's job. The winters are long, so that's hard, but mostly it's OK.

Oh.
Where do you live?
In Vermont.
Do you like it?
Well, the winters are long, but sure, it's fine.
Oh.
Where do you live now?
Burlington, Vermont. You've been there!
Oh, I have?
Do you like it?
Yes! It's just fine!
Oh. But where do you live?
In Vermont! And we love it!
Oh, I'm glad. Are you married?

Yes, to John. You like him.
Do you have any children?
It's strange to talk to my mother as if we are strangers. Besides, she was there when both children were born.
Yes, here comes one now!
Here's Helen! She's my baby!
Mama, can we go some-place?
Sure!
See these? These are no good.
Go put your shoes on and we can go.
OK.
That cute girl: is she yours?
Mama? Are you coming?

Here's a hike we could do— recommended for families— and it's not far—
It's forty five minutes away?
I'm not wasting my whole Saturday in the car.
We've been on every hike within thirty minutes of here—let's try something new.
No, not going.
Besides, I have my Magic tournament this afternoon.
Doesn't that cost money?
No allowance unless you go on this hike.
That's blackmail!
Exactly.
Way to make him want to go, Mama.

And, in order to earn that allowance, you also have to be cheerful.
Ok but I'm not sitting next to her.
I'm not sitting next to him.
Get in the damn Car!
Sure, I'll sit in the back.
But I'll still be able to hear him breathe!
Stop breathing!
Whoo-hoo! Family excursion!
FORTY-FIVE MINUTES LATER IN THE SMALL TOWN WHERE THE HIKE BEGINS...
OPEN
I'm hungry.
Oh look! The new book by ___!
I need some new bass strings.
Craft fair!
MARKET TODAY
PIZZA

Ten dollars is not too much for a hand-crocheted octopus, is it, Daddy?

Anyway, I'm allowed to waste my own money how I want.

Isn't it cute!

The trail is this way!

Are you going to ignore *me* and walk the whole way with *him*?

No, we're going to switch half way.

Half way? That's too long from now!

Oh and I'm Chopped liver?

You guys go ahead! We'll meet you back in town!

Sure?

OK!

Why do they call this "hiking"?

It's just the same as walking...

... except uphill, in the woods, with bugs.

How long have we been hiking?

22.5 minutes.

We'd better go back. I don't want Daddy and Helen to get mad waiting too long.

How was it?
Great. But we didn't make it to the top or see the water-fall that's supposed to be there.
Why did you come back so soon? This book just stopped being boring.
That was fun. Let's go home.
But — ice cream!
Cash, please.
Mama, you should get ice cream, too — it's your birthday.

KONN
HOTEL

What's in This bag? Anything for me?
Yeah! lots of chocolate chips.

I Thought we could make Cookies to bring to your Class on your birthday.

You're not saying anything. Don't you want to me to bring Cookies?
no.

What? Really? Why not?
They don't deserve it.

Good night.

Mama, wait!

What?

Do I have any questions, comments, or concerns?

Helen! Help!
You've got to save me from your brother!
He's chasing me!
He is cute, isnt he!
Eyeoo!

I have to do This homework but The instructions are in my science notebook That I left at school!

Let's see it. I'll help you.
You can't! All The questions are in That note-book!
CALL Peter!

He's at his dance class until 5.
Call Rosie.
She's in The other section.
Call Tess.
I'm not calling someone I don't know.
You've known her since 1st Grade! You used to play together!

A MINUTE LATER...
What about your home work?
I just rem-embered we'll have class time tomorrow to do it.
Are you sure it isn't just That you don't want to call any girls?

I lost my favorite socks on the farm field trip.
You do have a lot of worries tonight.
You don't have to worry about me or how fluffy I am!

Here comes Snowy on her cloud, towing another cloud!
Beep beep!

Here's what you do: put each worry onto the cloud I'm towing, and I'll fly it right out of Bunny World!
good bye, worries!

I wish it was that easy!
Now Snowy sails away to Kitty World where she makes it rain for 3 days.

Here's your heart line-look it connects with your head line- but your life line is separate.
On mine, it's The opposite! The heart line doesn't con-nect- except with The FATE Line. Maybe that's about how I met daddy!
What does mine mean?
Hmm.... I Think That you'll fall head over heals in LOVE.
AKK, I'm dying!
And if you look on The pinky side, The wrinkles tell you how many Children you will have... 5!
MOAN!

THE NEXT MORNING.
Mama, I've been studying my hands.
And it says right here in all The wrinkles who I'm going to marry.
Really? who?
Todd. A guy named Todd.
I hope Todd is nice and doesn't have a pot belly.
Now I don't have to worry about my future because I Know Todd is out There Waiting for me.
I'll carry on worrying for you Then.

Mama, do you have boobs?
You bet. That's where your food came from for your first year, remember?

No. Do I have boobs?
Not yet. You're only 8. They'll grow some time between 11 & 13.

Damn!
It's OK! It's good! All part of growing up!

I know, but that's right when I was planning to get my ears pierced & I don't want so much to happen all at once.

I dont want to grow boobs!
Oh well - It's part of Life.

Do you have Privates?
You Know I do! We all have Them!

Well, I dont want one!
That's funny - You talk about your privates all the time!

I just want a blank Space - like an American Girl doll.
I dont even want to pee!
You dont Think every American Girl doll's dream is to have a real private and to pee for real?

How about a lava lamp?
What is a lava lamp? Is it real lava?
BONK!
OW!
It came apart!
Mama! Are you OK?
I'm not sure it's a good idea for Noa's birthday present now.
I think she'd like it— only we'll get one in a box so it won't fall apart!
I'll just put this one back.
BONK!
OW!
Oh Mama!

Oh, OW! I have a headache now!
Are you sure a lava lamp is such a good idea for a birthday present? They seem so dangerous.
Now come along and sit in a comfy chair.
There, There, Mama.
I got hit on the head with a lava lamp twice but it doesn't matter because Helen took care of me.
Will you buy me that comfy chair?
No!

Enter your PIN when you're ready.
Kids, eh! Look at Them - brother and Sister - always at each other, aren't They!
Sure are.
But you're like "meh"! "This is my life."
Want a receipt?
Mama he's strangling me and you're not doing any Thing about it!
She started it!

Mama, want to do a quiz?
OK. What's it about?
Friends.
Are your friends Jocks or Brainiacs?
Brainiacs.
Are your friends smarter than you or are you smarter than them?
You have to answer!
They're smarter.
Would you rather have a group make-over party or a book-group?
What's the point of this quiz? When do we add up the score?
There is no score—it's just questions to discuss.
I'm not doing any quiz that doesn't tell me what cupcake or Greek goddess I am!

Mama, pick a bunny: Fiver, Snowy, Timothy, Inky, Ginger, Puffy, or Plum.
Fiver.

No, you can't pick Fiver!
Why not? What's This for?
A chose-Your-Own-Adventure for Bunnies. Chose another Bunny.

Snowy.
No, you can't chose Snowy, either.
Inky.
Why not Puffy? Puffy's a good choice!
If you won't let me chose Then why ask me?

Daddy! Mama can't decide which bunny—so will you pick one?
Any bunny As long as it's Puffy!

Mama look at This!
What is it?

It's my new glow-putty! Also, it's a portal into Bunny world.
Oh!

If it is, you'd better put the lid on it before you go to sleep or when you wake up your bed will be full of bunnies who have snuck Though!
Random Bunny-World bunnies?

Oh Mama, I don't have to worry about That!
Only bunnies who are already members can make it to my bed!
This is a very exclusive club.
Of about 20 pre-accepted bunnies!

Mama, can't you just please make me something to eat?
OK sure.
But I'd rather teach you how to make something you'd want to make.
Groan!
We don't always have to have a relationship where I make stuff for you! We could relate in whole new ways!
Why not just come right out and say you don't love me.
I do.
So, crackers & cheese?

Fret fret fret.
What's The matter, Helen?
Be calm! Lie down!
Groan. growl.

How can I when That white fluffy fabric we bought is getting un-fluffy and dingier by The day and we're not doing anything about it!
Oh

Let's make something out of it! A new bunny! A blanket, a pillow!
But then it will get all used up and not be fluffy any more!

We could Save The scraps in a Special drawer so they're allways stay fluffy.
OK
Wait—are you implying that I might not be as fluffy as I used to be?

Did you just pick something off that cup-cake and drop it on me?
Nod Nod
Why would you do that?
It was a piece of fuzz. You're fuzzy, so it must have been from you.

Oh Snowy Bunny, I love you!
I love you, too. Helen!

Of course I'm really saying I love you, Mama...
...for making Snowy come alive.

No, it's you who makes me come alive!
It's really you, Mama.

No it's you! Without you, I'd be a lifeless husk!
Oh no! Snowy fell asleep!
Well, It's late! Good night!

Bye, Mama! I'm leaving for School!

Bye, Helen! Wait-I'm coming with you!
No, Bunny, you stay here.
I can't bring you because There are boys There and I don't want Their big grubby hands on you.

Bye, Helen!

Bye, Helen.

Hi!Hi! What's That!
Really hot tea, Snowy Bunny - look out!

Huh! What's That you've got?
sniff sniff
Almond butter toast. Back up, snowy!

Snowy, you've got to give me some space when I'm eating -
PUSH
I wouldn't want to get any sticky jam on your nice white fur.

Snowy is in tears because you don't love her!
Would a bite of sticky carrot jam toast help?

Mama, will you say one of Those meditation Things That's suposed to help you fall asleep?
Sure.

The bunnies are all sitting around a crackling camp fire, watching The sparks spiral into The sky. Each bunny places a tiny worry on each spark and you all watch your worries disappearing into The night sky.

Gee, mama, your'e pretty good at That.
Really?
The bunnies are all calm now.
If That's really you.

Is That you, mama? Or a witch in disguise?
Cackle! Cackle!
Now I'll never get to sleep!

Pull The peach.
What peach?
This peach! My lower lip is like The Kind of peach Slice That Comes in a can.
You Know—the Kind of yellow peach slice That grandma Judy found stuck in her hair after The food fight in her College dorm.
yes—
Well, pull it!
Why?
It's what it's for. Pull the peach!

Snowy! Snowy Bunny! Where are you, bunny?
Mama, Snowy is lost.
Well, have you looked in your bed?
I Think so.
Helen help me! I'm lost!
Helen, where am I?
Look around, Snowy, and tell me what you see—Then we'll be able to find you.
I can't.
Why not?
It's all dark!
No, it's day! Did you fall down a well, Snowy?
No, but my paws are over my eyes—That's how lost I am!

Snowy! Take your paws away from your eyes and Then you'll see where you are!
I can't! I'm too Scared!
Now, Snowy. There's no reason to be afraid!
Oh yeah? There is too. You lost me!
I didn't lose you, bunny! You must have burrowed on Some-Thing.
Not on purpose!
It's just what bunnies do!
Snowy, you come out this minute!
Oh look! I was right here all along! You aren't going to punch me, are you?

Snowy! I would never punch you!
Really? Sometimes you get into a mighty temper!
I know, bunny- but I wouldn't take it out on you.
Sometimes bunnies can't help it...
Can't help what?
Well...
Burrowing and chewing... especially new things like your new bathing suit.

!!
Helen! Quick get up and look at The bunny in The yard! It's standing up on its hind legs!
Groan!
Why does that bunny have to bee There just when I wanted to sleep in?
Anyway I've seen bunnies before.
!!
I already Know how cute it is.
Tell it to go away.

Is This done?
You just took it out of The package one second ago.

Mama! I don't want you to get all old & rumply!
Ha! You & me both!

Under your chin is so soft and saggy like a lightly roasted marshmallow.
Hey, quit.

And The rest of your skin is like—
OK, enough already!

Mama! Come quick! Look!
What is it?

Aw, look at its little snout nibbling away!
It looks so soft!
Mama?
And it isn't in my garden!

Can I shoot it?

Hey! What are you doing? What's that?
chop chop
Watch out, Bunny-sharp.
What's This? Food for me? Want food!
Watch your nose, Bunny. Hot oil!
SCRAPE
Hold Bunny!
Bunny, Back off! I'm trying to make your dinner!
Bunny's DEAD!
Have a carrot, Bunny?

My parents still live in the house in Portland where I grew up.

My mom has Alzheimers. My dad takes care of her. It's only in the last four years that the disease has taken hold.

Before that my mom was a weaver. When I was in school I used to come home and would see her at her loom.

Her linen inlay tapestries hang in the Federal Court House in Portland and in many public and private collections across the country.

My dad is a painter and was a professor at the Pacific NW College of Art. He has shown his work since before I was born.

When we moved to this house I was seven years old.

It needed a lot of work but there was studio space for both parents. The house was built in 1907 at the time of the Lewis and Clark Exposition.

My dad's studio is on the 3rd floor. He put in two skylights overlooking the Industrial area (former site of a lake and The Exposition) and the Willamette River.

He makes paintings and constructions, often views of Italian and Portuguese gardens.

His compositions contrast the human-imposed order of gardens with the chaos of the natural world.

He works from photos he has taken on many trips to Europe.

He can't travel with my mother any more. Luckily he has a big archive of photos.

When I was little I used to lie in bed and hear him working until late: Pachelbel's Cannon and Django Reinhardt drifting through the heating vent.

My mom's studio was on the first floor in a sun-filled room off the living room.

She had two looms—one 10 feet long. The thumps of the beater shook the house and the rattle of the heddles as she changed the sheds was as familiar as rain.

She had a wall of spools of *linen thread* specially dyed. She used several strands of combined colors as she wove.

She drew her designs on graph paper and followed her drawings as she wove. Some tapestries required life-sized cartoons that she pinned under the warp. She couldn't see what the whole tapestry would look like until she took it off the loom.

Her designs play with the geometry of the tapestry grid and the dazzle effect of combining colors in warp and weft. A few years ago she stopped being able to follow her own designs and then to weave at all.

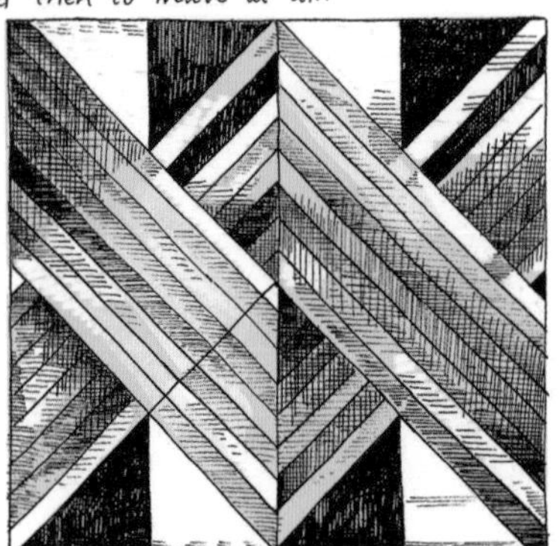

My parents gave the looms and most of the linen to the Oregon School of Art and Craft. Her studio is empty.

It didn't occur to me until I left to go to the University of Oregon that it was unusual to have two parents who made a living as artists.

Our neighborhood was full of artists. One house away from ours lived the Russos, a couple my grandparents' age.

Michele Russo was born in The USA but was stranded in Italy during his childhood during WWI. He was a painter, taught at the art school, and was active in arts organizations.

Sally Haley grew up in Connecticut, met Michele at Yale, married and moved to Portland in 1947.

They often had parties. I asked: "Why is everybody arguing?" Mike said, "Not arguing, discussing!" Sally made pizza, foccaccia, and cookies we loved.

When I was in art school in Portland, Sally tutored me in how to paint in egg tempera.

Mike and Sally's niece Laura founded a gallery in 1986 to show the work of Northwest artists, including my parents.

I worked at the gallery all through art school and the year before I left for grad school in Boston.

Mike, Sally, and Laura are all gone now. Martha Lee directs the gallery. My dad will have a show there in April.

A few houses past the Russos is Ursula Le Guin's house. We only ever saw her in passing.

I used to ride up and down the street on my bike with no hands. A friend teased me that I wanted Ursula Le Guin to see me and put me in a book.

I read her books on a sleeping porch facing west, overlooking the hills of Forest Park. I remember a rare clear twilight sky that made me ache with longing.

For what? The other worlds she wrote about in the Earthsea trilogy and in The Beginning Place? In that book there was also a twilit sky, but an eternal twilight rather than our ephemeral twilight that ends in night.

When I walked in the woods surrounding our neighborhood I always looked for traces of another civilization – an ancient ruin or a way through to another world.

My search lead me away from home and the familiar woods to the east, to Greece and Cyprus — another kind of Earthsea. But in this one, I could get a job. I drew artefacts from excavations, tiny mundane glimpses into another world.

I go back to Portland every year. This year we went in February for the kids' winter break.

The children like to come. They play hide and seek and hide where I used to hide.

They sleep in our childhood rooms and look at old photos that my mom put in albums and on the wall.

The house feels like home and home seems like it should last forever.

It can't and it won't.

I wish you'd go through and get rid of the books in your room. I don't want to have to do it alone.

You won't.

The jaws of my memory want to close on this house so hard.

I'll do it next time I'm here.

In April 2018, my children and I visited my parents for a week. In the mornings I went running in the woods.
Up Holman Lane...
...and down the Wild Cherry Trail to the Wildwood.
Here the city and family obligations seem far away,
and I feel closer to my childhood self,
and the feeling that it was possible that I could come across a mythical creature, another world, or a lost civilization.

Although the trails are well-travelled there are some places in these woods that seem as wild as if people have never arrived, and full of potential for other-worldly magic.
But then, as if to correct any illusion, around a turn of the Dogwood trail you suddenly hear the roar of the city and catch a glimpse of the river, bridges, and railroad.
The city has changed and grown since I moved away 20 years ago...
as well as circumstances of my life, but the woods continue, almost as if before time.
Once when I was 25 or so, I was running on the Wildwood, pretending to be one of the *immortals*— Artemis maybe—
swift footed huntress, daughter of Zeus—
When, suddenly a deer jumped across the path.

Certainly an epiphany! But of what spirit?
Of Artemis herself? A spirit of the free wildness of the woods.
But then I saw that the deer was jumping to her faun-
The deer was a mother, no avatar of a virgin goddess, even a goddess who presides over childbirth.
About ten years later, the deer lead me to find my own baby under a skunk cabbage.
Et Voila.

Just Kidding! I had to do it the hard way.
poof
And I never saw another deer in the woods again, avatar or not.
Now, everytime I run past this place on the trail where the deer jumped, I think of the goddess.
immortal, unchanging,
Huff huff
and by then I'm running in the direction of home, where my family, always changing, is waiting.
Hey Mama, make me an egg!

After the run and breakfast, it's time to take a walk with my mother.
I'd like to go out.
OK, I'll go with you.
She can't go out on her own. She would get lost.
Have you ever been down there?
Oh, sure.
What do you talk about with your mother when there is no past or future - or even much of a world beyond what she sees in front of her?
Look at those flowers.
I like to see them.
There's a dog.
Yes.
Where do you live?
In Vermont.
She asks this question over and over. She knows I don't live here.
Do you like it?
Sure.
Although she visited us in Vermont every year starting twelve years ago, it means nothing now.
Where do you live?
Vermont.
Do you have any like that?
Kids?
Sure! You know them.
I do?
She's taken care of them many times, including when I was away in Greece.
Let's go in there.

Chapman School.

Have you ever been in here?

My sister and I went to school here from when I was in second to eighth grade.

My mother made a tapestry for the school in 1990. She likes to visit it in the lobby but I'm not sure she knows why.

The linen inlay tapestry was one of several map tapestries she made for commissions. It shows prominent buildings, the river, streets, and parks of Portland. It also reveals her love for her adopted city, where my sister and I grew up.

If I say that they're dead she'll be sad.

She did get lost once and ended up downtown hours later. Police found her wandering vaguely and called my dad.

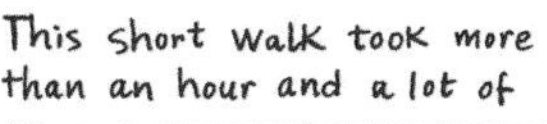
This short walk took more than an hour and a lot of energy.

Moving at her pace and only talking about things that won't confuse her is like being with a 3 or 4-year old child— a very sedate one.

Except I'm *her* child.

She must know on some level that she has daughters, even when we are not with her.

But she might not - maybe it's just vanity for me to think she does.

But she does know that I'm not usually here, I'm just visiting and must leave again. When she sees me she's aware that she will lose me.

For her, I must seem to exist in this moment only—and the moment is already gone.

When I leave, she won't be able to reach me (the phone doesn't make sense to her) and I become an ungraspable shadow.

Because she has lost herself, she has lost me as well.

We are both Demeter and both Persephone, both lost, both searching in the dark.

I want to stop time and hold onto her comforting body and the way she was before. But how?

And which moment would I capture? There is no one moment that could represent all the time she has been my mother.

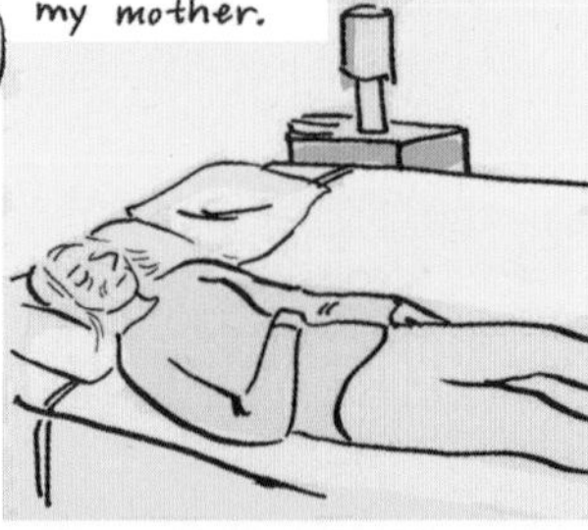

Without her memory, and my memories of her, and the memories of everyone who knew her, what is left?

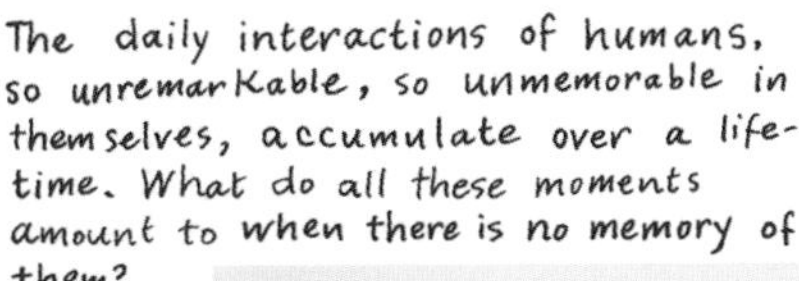

The daily interactions of humans, so unremarkable, so unmemorable in themselves, accumulate over a lifetime. What do all these moments amount to when there is no memory of them?

My grandmother Helen and me, age 1

My grandparents both had dementia, and now my mother. If this is hereditary, I'm next. I'm afraid.

My grand-parents, mother & aunt c.1959

Our small lives are so easily detached from our experiences, except in our attempts to record and create things that last.

my mother as a teenager

In May, for the past ten or so years, I've gone to Greece to draw pottery. Working with ancient artifacts gives me a feeling of connection to the people who made and used these objects.

My mother's tapestries show that once she had energy, intelligence, creative power, and skill. Her work is not only beautiful and intricate, but she made a living—what an example to follow.

When she first began to feel the effects of the disease she destroyed a lot of her older work. So she said, my sister and I would not have to deal with it.

Liz and I will inherit the work of our mother's whole life and our father's too. It's up to us to preserve - as we can.

Is there some comfort in the things humans make? My parents will not have graves to visit, but I will have her tapestries and my father's paintings to evoke their memories— if I remember.

Unless we humans create things that are lasting, the details of lives are gone in a generation. If there is solace in other peoples' stories, then it matters. Suddenly it matters very much!

When I was little, my mother wrote and illustrated a collection of stories from her and my dad's childhoods.

This is how I could tell my mother some of her own childhood stories. She recognized them but could not have told them herself.

This is to say, without the small memories that make up a life, what is life for? Maybe you wonder only when facing loss. But loss is around us all the time.

Yet we go on. We keep on making food & art, and driving our families crazy with nagging and hugging.

Each minute goes by, and more connections in my mother's brain disintegrate, but the strange bond of love — which I suppose holds the universe together — continues.